Original title:
The Garden Gate Poems

Copyright © 2025 Creative Arts Management OÜ
All rights reserved.

Author: Maxwell Donovan
ISBN HARDBACK: 978-1-80566-704-9
ISBN PAPERBACK: 978-1-80566-989-0

Lanterns of the Night

In the garden's nocturnal light,
Bugs do dance, much to my fright.
Worms wear coats, quite absurd,
And frogs croak jokes, so undeterred.

The moon's a lantern, glowing bright,
While gnomes hold parties, what a sight!
A raccoon steals snacks, oh what a pest,
Yet we all laugh, this place is best!

Petal-Paved Dreams

Petals blanket the ground below,
While bees in tuxedos put on a show.
Crickets serenade, no time for sleep,
As flowers gossip, secrets to keep.

Daisies chuckle, tulips sway,
While garden snakes dance away.
A squirrel on a unicycle rides,
As laughter echoes, our joy collides.

Threshold of Serenity

Step through the arch, what a surprise,
A llama in shades, oh how he pries!
Sunlight sparkles on dew-kissed grass,
As butterflies join a wobbly class.

The breeze whispers tales of delight,
While a tortoise races, what a sight!
In this realm where silliness thrives,
Every giggle ensures we're alive.

The Hidden Arbor

Behind the trees, there's a secret nook,
Where squirrels write mischief in a book.
A hedgehog in checkers thinks he's grand,
While veggies plan a music band.

The sun peeks in with a cheeky grin,
As flowers debate who'll wear the win.
With every chuckle, the shadows spin,
In this hidden spot, the fun begins!

Crossing the Boundary

A rabbit wears a little hat,
Sipping tea and chatting flat.
He's quite the gossip, funny chap,
Telling tales of a fox's nap.

But who would know, beneath the moon,
That toadstool dance is coming soon?
With fairies dressed in shiny lace,
They twirl and giggle, such a space!

The Hidden Sanctuary

Behind the hedge, a treasure trove,
Of socks and shoes the rabbits stole.
They laugh and chatter, what a sight,
   Hosting parties every night.

They serve cake made from flower dew,
With sprinkles that are sparkly blue.
Hiding crumbs in the lemon thyme,
A crunchy snack, oh, what a crime!

Butterflies on the Breeze

Butterflies in polka dots,
Debate the best of flower pots.
"Rose or daisy?" one does say,
"I prefer pink, it wins the day!"

They flit and flutter in the sun,
Making fun of how they run.
Wings so silly, dance and sway,
They giggle loud and fly away!

Where Wildflowers Wander

In fields where wildflowers' giggles blaze,
They dance around in playful ways.
With poppies blushing, daisies cheer,
They prance through all without a fear.

A squirrel joins in, a twirl and spin,
His fluffy tail, oh, what a win!
They laugh at clouds that join the fun,
A silly show, not yet begun!

The Other Side of Green

In a garden so neat and lovely,
Frogs croak jokes, oh so silly.
The flowers gossip in the breeze,
Talking about squirrels with big leaves.

A snail races, but oh dear me,
He forgot his map, lost in spree.
Bees buzz loudly, sharing sweet plans,
While ants play chess, with tiny hands.

The sun waves hello, bright and round,
Tickling daisies on the ground.
A hedgehog rolls in laughter's glee,
Tickling the grass, oh joyfully.

In this place, with humor so keen,
Life dances lightly, bright and green.

Petals on the Path

Petals tumble, graceful, bold,
Chasing butterflies in colors untold.
A dandelion plants a wee grin,
While worms play soccer with a spin.

The breeze carries a hat, oh so wide,
It lands on a rabbit, with nothing to hide.
Frogs wear glasses, trying to read,
The latest gossip from a seed.

Crickets sing silly tunes at night,
While fireflies twinkle with all their might.
Even the rocks are rolling in jest,
As laughter bubbles, it feels like a fest.

Petals on the path weave delight,
Making even grumpy toads feel bright.

A Time for Growth

In the pot where herbs do dance,
Basil whispers, 'Just take a chance!'
Thyme's plotting mischief, oh so sly,
While mint dreams big, reaching for the sky.

Carrots boast of lengths, oh my!
But radishes jest, 'Don't be shy!'
It's a root race, funny and loud,
In this patch, they're all quite proud.

Seedlings giggle, sharing their tales,
Of raindrops' journeys and summer gales.
With sunshine smiles, they wave and sway,
Finding joy in every playful day.

In a garden where laughter is grown,
It's clear that fun's the best-known.

Sunlit Reveries

Under sunbeams, dreams take flight,
Where daisies lounge, not caring what's right.
A lazy cat naps, dreaming of fish,
While a brave gopher makes a grand wish.

Clouds above are puffy and round,
As dreams tumble softly to the ground.
A butterfly trip, fancy and neat,
Lands right on a snail, oh what a treat!

Children giggle, chasing their tails,
While the hedgehogs tell their tall tales.
In this garden, with blooms so bright,
Fun finds you, day or night.

Sunlit reveries twirl and play,
In every nook, they find their way.

Whispers of the Wisteria

In a garden where flowers tell,
Wisteria whispers secrets well.
A squirrel in a top hat prances,
While daisies giggle, doing dances.

Beneath the blooms, a snail takes flight,
Claiming he's the garden knight.
Butterflies play tag with the bees,
While the roses laugh, 'Oh, please!'

Secrets Behind the Trellis

Behind the trellis, a rabbit plots,
To steal fresh carrots from the pots.
He talks of dreams, of golden cheese,
While cucumbers roll, laughing with ease.

A gnome peeks out with a cheeky grin,
Deciding today he might just win.
With marigolds wearing fancy hats,
They scheme, oh yes, just like old cats!

Echoes of the Moonlit Path

On a moonlit path, where shadows play,
A cat in a cape leaps, then sways.
The frogs are crooning a love song,
While crickets dance, all night long.

In the brambles, the owls roll their eyes,
At a hedgehog reciting cheesy lines.
The night is filled with silly cheers,
As laughter echoes, banishing fears.

Blooming Solitude

In solitude, a daisy dreams,
Of traveling wide with woolly seams.
She cracks jokes with a timid bee,
While petals flap, wild and free.

A cactus chuckles, sporting a smile,
While tinsel tulips strut in style.
The sun can't help but beam with glee,
At this odd garden comedy spree!

A Passage to Forgotten Dreams

A garden path that's lost in time,
Where daisies dance and robins chime.
I tripped on dreams, oh what a sight,
With gnomes who giggle in broad daylight.

The flowers plot a cheeky scheme,
To steal my hat, it seems a dream.
Their petals whisper, 'Come take a chance,'
As I tumble in my clumsy dance.

Still, in this plot, I find some cheer,
As weeds tell jokes that only I hear.
With every chuckle, I lose my way,
But who needs maps when jesters play?

So here I sit, a crown of blooms,
Kicked out of beds, and into rooms.
These zany plants, they made me see,
Even lost, I'm wild and free!

The Sound of Blossoming

In spring's embrace, the buds erupt,
With bees that bounce, and beetles plump.
The roses hum a poppy tune,
While violets spill their secrets soon.

The tulips boast of their fine flair,
While daisies giggle without a care.
A bloom with sass, a sunflower's grin,
Turns this park into a floral din.

The laughter swells as petals fall,
I tried to greet them, but missed the call.
With every step, a sprout or two,
Looks up and says, 'What's wrong with you?'

So down I plop, amidst the cheer,
The beauty blooms, absurd, sincere.
And though I fumble in this mess,
I'm laughing loud, wearing petals as dress!

Sunlight Through the Lattice

Sunlight spills through wooden beams,
While shadows play, creating dreams.
The marigolds wink and nod,
As I trip over a stray clod.

Each ray a giggle, bright and clear,
The garden whispers, 'Stay right here!'
But as I lean to breathe it in,
A bumblebee decides to spin.

He whizzes past, a buzzing ball,
I duck, I weave, I nearly fall.
Through tangled vines and hopping rays,
I chase the light on silly days.

In this delight of dancing sun,
I find my joy, I'm never done.
With every turn, I laugh and gloat,
Embraced by warmth, and pollen coat!

The Gatekeeper's Lament

Oh, I'm the gatekeeper, it's not so grand,
With squirrels at arms and a flower band.
I guard this entry with mismatched shoes,
While everything squabbles about the dues.

They scurry past with such great haste,
While I'm left here, my tea laid waste.
The hedgehogs argue, 'It can't be done!'
And all I can think is, 'This was not fun.'

A butterfly flutters, says 'What's your plea?'
I ask for silence, but they laugh at me.
With weeds in my hair and grass on my shirt,
I feel more like mulch than a gatekeeper's worth.

Still, here I stand, a twinkle-eyed host,
Amidst the chaos, I cherish the most.
For every giggle and furry parade,
Makes my duty a joyful charade!

Where Shadows Play

In the yard where shadows dance,
Lurking cats start a game of prance.
Squirrels plot their nutty schemes,
While the moon peeks through the beams.

Chattering frogs in a leafy band,
Sing ballads that are quite unplanned.
While the neighbor's dog looks on,
Snoring loudly from dusk till dawn.

Toadstools wear tiny hats so bright,
As fireflies flicker in the night.
A rabbit hops, quite out of tune,
Stepping on flowers, oh what a boon!

With giggles that echo near and far,
Even the chives join the bizarre.
A funny world where shadows lay,
Come out and laugh, there's fun to play!

A Portal of Color

Where bushes bloom in shades so wild,
The roses blush, the daisies smiled.
In daffodil dresses, twirls around,
A butterfly's waltz on grassy ground.

With tulips sipping morning dew,
They whisper secrets, just me and you.
A canvas brushed with laughter bright,
In petal land where dreams take flight.

Bees in tuxedos, buzzing around,
Waltzing madly, never bound.
Worms in shades of polka-dot,
Digging deep, dancing on the spot!

Oh, what a riot of color and cheer,
Pansies cracking jokes, loud and clear.
This garden of giggles, a joyful sight,
Where the sun chuckles, bringing delight!

Blooming Curiosities

Strange plants wiggle, do a jig,
With leafy hands, they dance so big.
Cacti wearing sunscreen coats,
While daisies play their tiny notes.

Sunflowers peek through the hedge so wide,
Giggling softly, never shy.
The garden gnomes with puzzled looks,
Search through flowers like curious books.

Petunias gossip, gossip all day,
Chatting about the garden play.
While carrots wear sunglasses and pose,
Pretending they're celebrities, who knows?

In this realm of blooming delight,
Nature's joy is a funny sight.
Curiosities sprout, wave, and sway,
Where laughter dances at every sway!

The Secret Passage

Behind the hedge, a doorway sly,
Leads to mischief, oh my oh my!
The littlest critters plot and scheme,
A hide-and-seek game, a crazy dream.

A hedgehog with glasses reads a book,
While ants in line take a sneaky look.
Toadstools host a tea party fair,
Where the cups are made of big ol' air.

Giggling fairies above the grass,
Sprinkle laughter as they pass.
A passage that spills joy and fun,
In sunlight stealing every pun.

So grab a friend, let's sneak away,
To discover the secrets of play.
Every plant and creature's a part of this,
In the passage of cheer, we can hardly miss!

The Frame of Forever

In a garden where daisies play,
A snail claimed the sun for the day.
With a hat made of leaves,
He danced 'round the eaves.

The flowers giggled at his parade,
While the ants waved their tiny spade.
They thought he was slick,
But he tripped on a stick.

A breeze blew and feathers took flight,
Causing him quite a fright.
He shouted, "Oh dear!
A chicken is near!"

But the wind just chuckled with glee,
As the snail rolled back under the tree.
With a wink and a sigh,
He said, "Not goodbye!"

Whispers in the Winds

The wind blows through the tulips bright,
Whispering secrets, a quirky delight.
"Why did the flower wear a frown?
Because it lost its crown!"

A butterfly giggled, flapping its wings,
Stirring up laughter from all garden things.
"Let's throw a bash,
With pollen and ash!"

The bees hummed a tune, busy and bold,
Sharing honey tales, sweetly retold.
"Who tickled the cat,
That made it go splat?"

So the garden erupted with joy,
Each insect and bloom played along like a toy.
It's a whimsical scene,
In this vibrant green sheen.

Whispers Beyond the Threshold

Beyond the gate where shadows play,
A frog is a jester; hip-hip-hooray!
He croaks out a joke,
With a wink and a poke.

"Why don't frogs like fast food?" he quips,
"Because they're afraid of the long trips!"
The fireflies giggle,
As the crickets wiggle.

The hedge whispers secrets, oh so sly,
"Did you hear about the bee who could fly?
He couldn't find home,
Just roamed and roamed!"

Yet laughter ensued throughout the night,
With shadows dancing, a charming sight.
In the moon's soft glow,
More giggles would flow.

Secrets in the Bloom

In a patch of tulips, purple and gold,
A bee found a sweet tale to be told.
"Did you know that the garden gnome,
Claims he's just here to roam?"

He considered himself quite the sage,
With stories that reeked of age.
"Once I met a cat,
Who danced with a rat!"

The daisies all leaned in to hear,
Giggling softly, full of cheer.
"Oh go on, dear friend,
This tale has no end!"

But the gnome fell asleep, what a sight!
Dreaming of merry moonlit nights.
With secrets and dreams,
In this garden of beams.

Curls of Ivy

In a garden where the weeds dance,
A squirrel steals a seed with a glance.
The sun tickles leaves with a wink,
While bees buzz by, too busy to think.

A pair of shoes left on the lawn,
Are now a throne for a rebellious fawn.
With laughter echoing through the trees,
It's a party here, with everyone at ease.

The flowers wear hats of yellow and red,
As butterflies frolic on a flower bed.
A snail takes a selfie, so proud and slow,
While ants march by in a perfect row.

In this garden, giggles take flight,
As frogs in tuxedos croak through the night.
Curls of ivy twist in a playful dance,
In a world where smiles get the last chance.

A Sanctuary of Solitude

A chair made of twigs creaks with a sigh,
While a lazy cat dreams, stretched out nearby.
In the shade of the trees, where time moves slow,
A gnome holds court, but no one can know.

Bugs throw a party; it's quite the charade,
While one flies in circles, losing its way.
The flowers giggle as they bloom so wide,
In this sanctuary where secrets reside.

A crow tells jokes that only it finds funny,
Sipping on dew, oh so sweet and runny.
The breeze whispers tales of ancient sprites,
In a calm corner where laughter ignites.

And in this quiet, a frog gives a cheer,
For a snail that's won the race of the year.
What a sight, this solitude's grace,
As silly creatures frolic, keeping pace.

Secret Trails of Peace

Along the winding paths where daisies peek,
A tortoise claims victory, though he's quite weak.
Blades of grass tickle his chin with delight,
While crickets chirp under the moon's soft light.

A butterfly flutters with flair and finesse,
While worms compose tunes; it's quite the mess.
In this serene space, laughter's the star,
As puddles reflect the dreams from afar.

The trees gossip softly, their leaves having fun,
Sharing wild secrets 'til the day is done.
While shadows play tag in a playful parade,
Life here is silly, never afraid.

And when the sun sets, a party begins,
With fireflies twinkling like stars with their fins.
In secret trails where the whimsical roam,
Each step taken feels just like home.

Tender Footsteps

In a patch kissed by light, where joy often springs,
A puppy prances, chasing fluttering things.
With each tender footstep, he makes quite the mess,
As giggles escape from a garden's caress.

A ladybug lounges, legs crossed with style,
While ants in a line get lost in a pile.
The daisies nod, sharing puns with the breeze,
As sunlight filters through the swaying trees.

Here, laughter is a potion, brewed with such care,
As clouds float by, adding fluff to the air.
With every soft step, bright spirits arise,
In this place of delight, life wears a disguise.

So come for a dance with the moon's silver light,
Join frogs with their banter till the stars are bright.
In tender footsteps, let joy take a stake,
Finding fun in each corner, make no mistake.

Embracing the Wild

In the thicket, squirrels dance,
Chasing shadows, a wild romance.
A rabbit hops, spots a snail,
"Excuse me, sir, you've lost your trail!"

Mice and birds engage in jest,
"How many seeds can you digest?"
While butterflies laugh, flitting by,
"Don't mind me, just learning to fly!"

A raccoon wears a clever grin,
Practicing winks, where to begin?
The ants have a meeting, quite profound,
Discussing crumbs they've recently found.

So let's join in this quirky spree,
Nature's laugh is wild and free.
With each step through this buzzing land,
You might just find your own silly stand.

Stories in the Soil

Worms hold tales, if you listen close,
About the rain and the damp, they boast.
"Last night we had a party, oh my!
With the mud pies, we reached for the sky!"

A ladybug shares a secret or two,
"I fell in a puddle, but I made it through.
The grasshoppers cheered, it was quite the sight,
As I styled my polka dots just right!"

But watch out for that old, grumpy mole,
"Stop your ruckus, I'm trying to roll!"
Yet even he chuckles at a thistle's plight,
"Could you kindly take that ruckus to the night?"

Under the soil, stories thrive,
In laughter and chaos, the garden's alive.
Let's dig in together, embrace the fun,
In this loamy life, there's room for everyone!

The Bough's Gaze

High up where the branches meet,
The birds gossip, a tweet-tweet treat.
"Did you see how the cat did trip?
All that fuss over one tiny slip!"

A squirrel nods, munching a nut,
"Just last week, I saw him strut.
But oh, how he jumped and fled—
With a leaf on his head, he surely bled!"

The boughs sway in their leafy delight,
Creating a stage, a comical sight.
"Come one, come all, let's make a fuss!
Take a seat, throw out the bus!"

The rustle of leaves is laughter's espouse,
Under the boughs, merriment arouse.
So gaze with me at this humorous spree,
Nature's own show, infinitely free!

A Canopy of Whispers

Underneath a leafy dome,
A choir of critters call it home.
"Did you hear the bee's little joke?
He buzzed his way through a cloud of smoke!"

The frogs croak back, "That's quite absurd!
All we do is croak, have you heard?"
While a witty owl smirks with glee,
"Monotonous life? Not for me!"

Beneath this canopy, laughter spills,
From stories of ants and their little drills.
So sit, dear friend, this time we'll spend,
In nature's laughter, our spirits will mend.

In a world so wild, in a hush so bright,
Find joy in whispers and dance in the light.
For every leaf holds a chuckle and cheer,
A reminder that joy's always near!

Stories in the Stems

In a patch where doodlebugs roam,
Carrots tell tales, then laugh and foam.
Radishes dance with a jittery jig,
While tomatoes gossip, oh so big!

Bugs wear hats, they shine and prance,
Making every sprout Do a silly dance.
Cucumbers chuckle, the peas poke fun,
In this garden, joy has just begun!

A sunflower winks, a shade of glee,
While carrots play truth or dare with a bee.
Petunias giggle, what a sight to behold,
Planting the secrets, never growing old!

So come and enjoy this vibrant scene,
Where laughter blooms, and all is serene.
In every stem, stories thrive and sway,
Join the fun and throw worries away!

Sprouts of Thought

In the corner where the beans hang tight,
Radical thoughts take root, what a sight!
Peas debate if they should roll or stack,
While corn's planning a popcorn attack!

The herbs discuss the latest trends,
Mint rolls its eyes, as basil pretends.
Cilantro chimes in with a spicy claim,
While parsley just goes on with its game!

A lettuce leaf poses for the gram,
Cabbage is jealous, wants to be glam.
Kale throws shade, with a twist of fate,
In this wacky world, they just can't wait!

From sprouts of thought, wisdom grows tall,
In this chatty harvest, it's a hoot for all!
So lean in close and hear their cheer,
In the funny realms, nothing's unclear!

Woven Moments

In a vine where whispers twist and turn,
Lettuce giggles, while onions yearn.
Radishes weave their colorful thread,
Bouncing ideas like they're being fed!

Daisies tell stories of dreams they chase,
While the broccoli's lost in a funny face.
Zucchini rolls by with a wink of surprise,
Knitting moments beneath sunny skies!

Fertilizer gossip drifts on the breeze,
Telling secrets under leafy trees.
With each woven stroke, hilarity flows,
In a garden where nobody knows!

Every twist and turn, a moment to share,
With laughter and joy filling the air.
Let's celebrate life in colors so bright,
In these woven moments, pure delight!

Echoes of the Fern

Beneath the fronds where chuckles bloom,
Ferns whisper secrets, dispelling gloom.
With every rustle, there's laughter around,
In this leafy haven, joy is profound!

"We'll throw a party," the ferns declare,
"Bring your pals from the forest, we'll pair!"
The mushrooms are in, dressed like the stars,
Spreading good vibes from Jupiter to Mars!

With thyme on the playlist, and minty cheer,
Clover brings kicks as the dance draws near.
In the echo of whispers, joy will not fade,
As nature's chorus plays, a grand charade!

Amidst the ferns where fun takes flight,
Giggling shadows dance in delight.
In this sprightly grove, laughter will churn,
Join the merry echoes of the fern!

Dance of the Shadows

In the garden, shadows prance,
Chasing sunlight with a dance.
A squirrel spins, the flowers giggle,
While bees buzz in, a happy wiggle.

The daisies laugh, the lilies cheer,
A frog jumps in, oh dear, oh dear!
The mushrooms wiggle, wearing hats,
As shadows play with friendly cats.

But wait, a gust! The breeze is sly,
It steals a hat, oh my, oh my!
The shadows tumble, trip, and roll,
In this madcap, jolly stroll.

With every step, mistakes ensue,
A butterfly steals the gardener's shoe.
Laughter echoes in the glade,
As nature's antics make the shade.

Snapshots of Sunlight

A camera clicks, and flowers pose,
With silly faces, who really knows?
Sunbeams peek through leaves so green,
Capturing moments pure and keen.

A bee hitches a ride on a rose,
Saying, "Cheese!" while striking a pose.
The daisies wink with cheeky grins,
As sunlight dances, the laughter begins.

Snap! A cloud makes a funny face,
All the raindrops join in the race.
They giggle and splash on the petals bright,
Creating a scene of pure delight.

The sun sets down with a wink so sly,
As the flowers hum a sleepy lullaby.
In this garden, joy never ends,
With each snapshot, nature's best friends.

Portraits in Petals

Petals gathered, colors swirl,
Creating portraits in a twirl.
A sunflower frowns, it's not quite right,
While violets blush in morning light.

The roses pout, taking their cue,
Saying, "We're just too good for you!"
Tulips giggle, tipping their hats,
"Oh, please, don't mind the garden chats!"

Snap a selfie with the ferns,
As the dandelions take their turns.
A beetle strikes a pose with flair,
While ladybugs float through the air.

Each flower shows off its best side,
With green leaves acting as their guide.
In this gallery of nature's smiles,
Every petal bursts with funny styles.

Lavenders of Memory

A lavender field waves to the sun,
Whispering secrets of laughter and fun.
The bees remember when they danced,
And the butterflies flit, a chance romance.

Each bloom holds tales of ticklish days,
With breezes blowing in a playful haze.
The bunnies hop in a silly race,
As the daisies fold their petals with grace.

Memories scented, oh, what a blend,
With giggles echoing around each bend.
Sweet lavender laughs, swirling around,
In this fragrant haven, joy is found.

Yet as twilight wraps its gentle shroud,
The memories linger, soft and loud.
In lavender dreams, we start to sail,
With a smile in our hearts, we cannot fail.

Beneath the Canopy

Beneath the leafy shade, we play,
Where squirrels dance and children sway.
A frog in a hat does a silly jig,
While ants march by, oh so big!

We laugh at bees that buzz around,
And trip on roots buried in the ground.
A sunflower winks, its petals wide,
As we hide from the rain, in glee we bide.

Butterflies wear colors that astound,
While worms dig deep, not making a sound.
Petunias gossip, oh what a sight,
As we sip our juice, things feel just right.

In this playful nook, time flies by,
Let's plant some jokes, let laughter spry.
With snickers and giggles, we'll fill the air,
Beneath the canopy, without a care.

Radiance of the Dawn

At dawn's first light, the roosters crow,
A cat in a sunbeam steals the show.
Dew drops twinkle like diamonds bright,
While daisies chuckle in morning light.

The garden is waking, and so are we,
As bugs in tuxedos sip morning tea.
A worm in a bow tie offers a toast,
To all the blooms, the ones he loves most!

With a wink from a sunflower, we start to sing,
The chorus of blossoms, oh what joy they bring!
Petals turn pink and then back to green,
Sprinkling laughter in each little scene.

As the sun climbs high, shadows do play,
A dance of delight, on this funny day.
With giggles and grins, we paint the morn,
In the garden's embrace, we feel reborn.

Echoes of Blossoms

In the garden where giggles float,
Echoes of blossoms, on merriment they wrote.
A rose tells jokes to the starlit night,
While the nightingale hums with pure delight.

Here daisies prance in a fluffy dress,
And violets boast of their soft finesse.
With whispers of petals, secrets unfold,
In this lush rendezvous, so merry and bold!

The tulips tap dance in the breeze so light,
As a bumblebee buzzes and takes its flight.
"Knock, knock!" they shout, with giggles galore,
"Who's there?" we ask, "Just blooms at the door!"

With echoes of laughter in petals we find,
The joy of the garden plays tricks on the mind.
In this realm of cheer, let your heart take root,
Among echoes and whispers, life's really a hoot!

Beyond the Climbing Roses

Beyond the climbing roses, a mischief brews,
A rabbit sings ballads and a goose wears shoes.
The bumblebee struts with a crown of gold,
Whispering tales that never grow old.

We giggle at daisies who play peek-a-boo,
While clouds sail by, dressed in shades of blue.
Sunshine paints laughter on petals so bright,
And cucumbers chuckle at their silly plight.

The hedgehog twirls in a pirouette,
While ladybugs cheer, they're not done yet!
With jokes that sprout in the warm sunshine,
Every moment here feels simply divine.

So let's wander this path where the whimsy thrives,
With nature's own humor, we feel so alive!
Beyond the climbing roses, let giggles abound,
In this funny garden, joy knows no bounds.

Nurtured by Nature

In the garden where daisies dance,
A gnome spins tales with every glance.
Worms wear shades, sipping on tea,
Bumblebees buzz in glee, oh me!

Rabbits hop with stylish flair,
Telling secrets without a care.
The carrots tease from their patch,
While the broccoli starts a rap batch.

Sunflowers gossip about the rain,
Petunias hum a silly refrain.
Beetles break dance on a leaf,
Each flower shares its joyful belief.

Underneath the moonlit skies,
Even the crickets wear surprise.
In this patch of mirth and cheer,
Nature's laughter echoes clear.

The Secret of the Seeds

I found a seed that whispered right,
It said, "Plant me! I'll take flight!"
A sprout emerged with a hat of green,
Claiming to be the garden's queen.

Radishes wore a blush of red,
While peas in pods danced ahead.
Tomatoes sported a cheeky grin,
Saying, "We'll win this race, let's begin!"

The beans began to twirl about,
While pumpkins sang, 'We have no doubt.'
Each plant had wild stories to weave,
In this green land, you won't believe!

As dusk fell with a playful sigh,
Stars winked down, oh my, oh my!
Secrets lingered in the breeze,
The garden giggled with perfect ease.

Wandering through Wonder

A path of petals, soft and bright,
Leads me through a new delight.
With every step, giggles play,
As flowers beckon, 'Come this way!'

Butterflies throw a fancy ball,
Waltzing past a toad's warm call.
The daisies wear their fancy shoes,
While snails slide by, sharing the news.

The grass tickles my bare toes,
While squirrels debate the best of shows.
A hedgehog recites a short rhyme,
Embracing the joy of this silly time.

Under a tree with a swing so wide,
I laugh with the shadows, letting them glide.
In this wonderland of giggles and fun,
Every moment feels like a sunny run.

Mosaic of Time

Each flower holds a story fine,
Unraveling threads of summer's shine.
The daisies whisper tales of yore,
While leaves dance with legends galore.

A beetle claims to be a knight,
Guarding blooms with all its might.
Sunsets paint the sky with glee,
As shadows stretch for a little spree.

The seasons laugh in playful jest,
Trading stories, doing their best.
With every petal, a memory made,
In this vibrant tapestry, none can fade.

As twilight wraps the garden's glow,
Laughter lingers, soft and slow.
Each moment stitched, a patchwork tune,
A hilarious dance beneath the moon.

Mosaic of Greens

In the garden, weeds unite,
They hold a dance, quite the sight.
One says, 'Hey, pull me, please!'
But they giggle in the breeze.

Rabbits in dapper hats collide,
They race the snails, quite the ride!
Caught in a carrot caper,
What fun to be a veggie taper!

Ladybugs wear tiny shoes,
Rediscovering old garden blues.
Among the petals, they prance around,
Finding fashions in the ground.

So here's a toast to all that grows,
Whispers in the rows of prose.
Life's a joke wrapped in green,
In this space of silly scene.

Twilight's Threshold

As dusk settles on the yard,
Fireflies start their evening card.
One old bug with a bright flair,
Says, 'Do you dance, or just stare?'

Frogs croak tunes with odd notes,
While crickets wear little coats.
A bat zooms in, with a swoosh—
'Mind the gap!'—as he rushes!

The moon, a giant silver coin,
Loses its shine without a groin.
Each shrub whispers punchlines sweet,
As nocturnal guests take a seat.

So gather near as shadows bloom,
Let laughter fill the airy room.
Under stars that twinkle bright,
We celebrate this comical night.

Mysteries of the Arbor

Beneath the tree, secrets loom,
Squirrels plot their next big boom.
One says, 'Hide the acorn stash!'
The others giggle, 'Make a dash!'

Branches sway with gossip tales,
While wind doth spin its windy gales.
A wise old owl, with a wink,
Says, 'Do you ponder, or just think?'

Bumblebees buzz like tiny cars,
Arguing over who's the star.
In the shade, shadows play games,
Chasing whispers, calling names.

So climb the roots and sing along,
In this haven, where hearts belong.
Mysteries laughter hides within,
Stories waiting, let's begin!

The Blooming Door

A door that blooms with flowers bright,
Opens wide to sheer delight.
Inside, the pots share funny lore,
Each plant a tale, they can't ignore.

Petunias prank with vibrant laughs,
While daisies offer young photographs.
'Look at me!' the tulips shout,
As garden gnomes begin to doubt.

Sunflowers wear the sun's warm dress,
Winking as they aim to impress.
'Oh darling, hold that pose!' they plead,
For nature knows the art of need.

So swing that door and jump inside,
Where every plant is laughs and pride.
In this jolly patch, so divine,
The bloom sings sweetly, 'You're all mine!'

Heartstrings in the Daisy

In the garden, laughter grows,
Daisies dance in silly rows.
A bumblebee with quite a grin,
Sips from cups, let the fun begin.

The sun winks at a floppy hat,
While squirrels organize a chat.
They trade secrets, hidden treats,
Underneath the daisy seats.

A rabbit hops, a jolly leap,
Whispers to the flowers, 'Don't sleep!'
A ladybug, red and spry,
Tells a joke that makes birds fly.

With each petal, joy expands,
As nature sings with gentle hands.
In this patch of bright delight,
Heartstrings tug, what a funny sight!

Roots of Reflection

In the soil, the jokes take root,
Worms tell stories, ain't that cute?
With a wink, they dig and laugh,
Planting seeds for a hearty half.

Old trees gossip, branches sway,
Sharing tales of yesterday.
A squirrel wearing glasses wide,
Reflects on nuts he tried to hide.

The bumblebees buzz a tune,
Underneath the silver moon.
"Hey there, roots, why so deep?"
"Because we're tired, let us sleep!"

Even daisies twist with cheer,
Roots of laughter drawing near.
In this patch, where humor shines,
Reflection grows on sunny lines!

Garden of Echoes

In the garden, echoes play,
Whispering secrets of the day.
A frog croaks tales so profound,
While daisies giggle all around.

The sunbeams tickle leaf and stem,
Creating chuckles—a real gem.
The echoes bounce from tree to wall,
It's like a joke that charms us all.

A parrot in its feathery coat,
Mimics laughter, what a note!
As butterflies flit on colored wings,
They join in on the joy that springs.

In this vibrant, echoing place,
Every bloom wears a smiley face.
So let the echoes roam and blend,
For laughter is a never-end!

Fragrance of the Forgotten

In the corner, scents arise,
Whispers of the past, oh my!
Lavender giggles with delight,
While herbs share tales late at night.

Petunias sing of days gone by,
In scented breezes, laughter sighs.
A rogue vine, with mischief rife,
Clusters tales of garden life.

Chives chuckle as they sway,
A playful breeze joins in the fray.
"What's the joke?" the rosemary asks,
"Just root for me in all my tasks!"

In this patch of fragrant dreams,
Everyone's bursting at the seams.
For the forgotten, they impart,
A funny scent to every heart!

The Enchanted Threshold

At the gate where laughter dwells,
A squirrel begs for cookie spells.
The flowers wear their brightest hats,
While gnomes debate the best of cats.

A rabbit steals a sunny seat,
Claiming it, oh what a feat!
The fence posts gossip with great cheer,
About the bugs that wander near.

The butterflies throw quite the dance,
As bees all buzz and weave their trance.
With every laugh that fills the air,
You wonder if the sun's aware.

So step right up, don't miss the show,
Where everything might just say "hello!"
In this realm, the silliness flows,
And even garden gnomes strike poses!

Petals of Reflection

In a patch where daisies grin,
And beetles wear their little skin,
The daisies talk of who's more bright,
While pansies gossip, out of sight.

They check their mirrors made of dew,
Comparing petals, red to blue.
The tulips giggle, what a sight,
As vines all twist in sheer delight.

The sun confesses a tiny blush,
While grasshoppers hop, oh what a rush!
Each bud has dreams of sprouting tall,
While daisies form a giant brawl.

With petals twirling in the breeze,
Who knew a garden could tease?
Every leaf holds dreams and schemes,
Laughing wildly in sunlit beams.

Secrets of the Ivy Vines

The ivy whispers secrets low,
To every worm that wanders slow.
It tells of twirls and twists so grand,
While snails plot with the mossy band.

With tendrils dressed in emerald lace,
They hide from winds, a cozy place.
The bugs beneath are wise and sly,
While ivy holds its breath and sighs.

A chameleon waits, a silly feat,
To blend in with the rolling beat.
As flowers giggle, sharing tales,
Of adventures in the garden trails.

So if you wander, just take heed,
The ivy knows where laughter leads.
Join the fun, don't be shy,
In these green halls, you'll surely fly!

Beneath the Canopy

Underneath the leafy dome,
A caterpillar makes its home.
It dreams of wings and soaring high,
While chirping crickets make it sigh.

Squirrels play tag in sunlight beams,
Creating chaos, chasing dreams.
The clouds all peek, a game of hide,
While flowers bloom with great pride.

A turtle winks with crafty glee,
As dragonflies buzz merrily.
With every rustle, laughter hides,
In every nook, where fun abides.

So come and join this leafy lot,
Where silliness and joy's the plot.
Underneath this vibrant shade,
Every giggle gets remade!

Pathways of Petals

In a garden so grand, where the flowers all play,
The roses wear hats, in a fine cabaret.
The daisies do jive, while the tulips do sing,
They dance in the sun, what a joyful thing!

The bees in their suits buzz a chorus so sweet,
While ants in a line march to their own beat.
The squirrels tell jokes, with their acorn-filled cheeks,
While the butterflies giggle—oh, such funny freaks!

The fountains spit water like a hiccup or snort,
The frogs in their croaks hold a comedy sport.
Down pathways of petals, all merry and bright,
This whimsical world is a pure delight!

So stroll through this garden, let laughter abound,
Where petals are giggles that float all around.
With humor and cheer in this flowery place,
Every step is a chuckle, a smile on your face!

Enchanted Entry

At the enchanted entry where mischief ignites,
The shrubs tell tall tales of fantastical nights.
The gnomes in their caps hold a council bizarre,
Debating the best way to chase off a star!

The flowers wear sneakers, they sprint 'round the bend,
While the veggies hold races, they'll never defend.
The cabbage calls out, "I'm the fastest of greens!"
And lettuce just giggles, revealing its seams!

A hedgehog recites rhymes as he bounces along,
While the crickets compose an adventurous song.
A swirl of excitement, a sparkle of fun,
In this whimsical entrance, the laughter's begun!

With each turn of a leaf, there's a secret to share,
And if you lean close, there's delight in the air.
So step through the threshold of jocular care,
The entry's enchanted, with joy everywhere!

Gateways to Wonder

Through gateways to wonder, where silliness thrives,
The daffodils gossip about all their five lives.
The sunflowers pose like celebrities grand,
With selfies and smiles—just as they have planned!

The mischievous squirrels with their acorn-filled hats,
Trade secrets in whispers, avoiding the cats.
A raccoon in shades claims he's surfing the breeze,
While the pigeons just laugh, saying, "Chill, if you please!"

From corners of color, the giggles erupt,
As vines weave together a comedy cup!
The cherries swing low, on a bright frosty vine,
Declaring, "Come join us! This garden's divine!"

With petals a'flutter, and moonbeams of light,
These gateways to wonder keep spirits so bright.
And as laughter takes bloom, on this fancy escapade,
Every moment of joy is uniquely displayed!

Flora's Embrace

In Flora's embrace where the blooms share a jest,
The cacti wear glasses to look their best.
The lilies hold court, full of posh and delight,
While the windchimes giggle, swaying left and right!

With petals like pillows that bounce to the beat,
The daisies play hopscotch beneath our feet.
The thorns, though quite prickly, have stories to tell,
Of evening adventures they've had—oh so swell!

The tomatoes roll dice, at a game of chance,
While worms do the tango, oh what a dance!
A hedgehog, quite humorous, jests with a grin,
"How many tickles does it take to make kin?"

So sit in this garden of laughter and grace,
Where Flora's embrace brings a smile to your face.
In a world filled with color, where joy intertwines,
There's magic and humor in Nature's designs!

Starlit Strolls

With stars above, we make our way,
Chasing fireflies till the break of day.
"My shoes are squeaky," I laugh and shout,
As we twirl around, our worries tossed out.

In a crooked path, we stumble and fall,
Trying to catch that moonlit ball.
"Did you see that!" I point with glee,
It's just my shadow; oh, woe is me!

The grass tickles our toes, oh what a scene,
We dance like we're in the latest magazine.
"Who needs a map?" I cheerfully cry,
As a hedgehog rolls by giving me a sly eye.

The picnic blanket waits with treats galore,
But first let's unwrap that glittering roar.
"Is it wine or grape juice?" you slyly tease,
"Just your imagination!" I giggle with ease.

Journey to the Hidden Veil

We set out bright, with a map in hand,
Searching for secrets in this mystic land.
But lo and behold, a wild goose chase,
"Oh look! A turtle!" I giggle and race.

The veil hangs low, with whispers and laughs,
"Knock knock!" says a rabbit, "Who drafts these paths?"
We follow the sparkles, through thickets and thorns,
Finding surprises in the tangle of morns.

A tree swings low, our laughter it sways,
"Wouldn't it be neat if trees had toupees?"
The babbling brook claps its wings in delight,
As we prance and twirl through the soft dusk light.

Finally there lies a glimmering show,
Is it treasure or just the old garden gnome?
"Let's dance with this thing, it can't possibly bite!"
The gnome just grumbles, "I've napped here all night!"

The Sylvan Entrance

At the edge of the woods, the signs are quite bold,
"Enter at your risk, there are stories untold!"
With a wink and a grin, I push through the vines,
Can there be trolls? I promise they'll dine!

"Look, a squirrel in a top hat!" I squeal,
It's just a pine cone, but isn't that real?
With every rustle, we jump and we squeak,
It's a leaf! It's a twig! Let's have a peek!

In this sylvan delight, with mischief afoot,
Who knew stick figures could cause this much soot?
"Do trees have feelings?" you boldly inquire,
As I climb to the top of a very small spire.

We find an old bench, our moment to rest,
"Were there knots in these woods? We could get blessed!"

But instead it's a gopher who snorts with a wink,
"Adventures are better when you can just blink!"

Serenity in the Corners

In the corners of life, the laughter spills out,
Where squirrels gossip and trees strain to shout.
"We could build a fort!" you bright-eyed declare,
With leaves as our walls, we'll shelter with care.

A butterfly giggles, darting through space,
"Oh my goodness! This won't fit in my case!"
We chase it around, as it leads us with glee,
To a patch of wildflowers that beckon us free.

But what's this? A mushroom with freckles so bright,
"Could it be magic?!" I gasp with delight.
It dances and twirls; is it here for the show?
"You're just out of luck, let's leave it to grow!"

So we sprawl in the grass, our dreams take to flight,
With giggles and whispers, we banish the night.
In corners of bliss, we find silly plays,
In gardens of joy, we'll dance through our days.

Fractal Flora

In a garden so neat, with flowers in rows,
A daisy joked hard, as the tulip just froze.
"Why was the mushroom invited to play?"
"Because he's a fungi, and brightens the day!"

With lettuce all laughing, and carrots in suits,
They threw a big party, with jellies and roots.
A gnome with a grin shared his jokes in the sun,
And even the compost began having fun!

The roses were twirling, they danced all around,
While the daisies held hands, and they spun on the ground.
The violets whispered, "Let's play tag tonight,"
Then fell in a heap as they giggled with delight!

Oh, what a scene, with a frog on a swing,
He croaked out a tale of a golden-haired king.
While bees buzzed in chorus, they joined in the cheer,
In this fractal of laughter, the joy was quite clear!

Twilight's Embrace

In the dusk of the eve, when the fireflies play,
A raccoon in a tux said, "What's on today?"
He juggled some acorns, made everyone clap,
While the owl offered snacks, set a feast on a lap.

The sun took a bow, as the stars came to blink,
The moon dressed in pajamas, raised a glass for a drink.
"Let's toast to the dusk, to the critters we meet,
And to dancing with shadows, on soft, grassy feet!"

The hedgehogs were twirling with top hats so spry,
While the cantankerous cat simply strolled by.
He sneezed at the chorus, then joined in the song,
As the night grew adventurous, where all could belong.

With laughter and giggles, the twilight hung tight,
As the world spun in circles, all merry and bright.
So come take a seat, on this cushion of moss,
In Twilight's embrace, nothing is ever a loss!

Mind the Hedge

A squirrel on a sign said, "Watch where you tread!"
As rabbits made mischief with crumbs on your bed.
They piled up the snacks, like a banquet of joy,
While hedges just hummed with a whimsical ploy.

Now gardeners grumbled, as weeds had a ball,
While ladybugs dressed up, playing catch in the hall.
With petals like confetti, they paraded with flair,
Proclaiming, "Oh darling, there's fun everywhere!"

The hedges formed whispers, of secrets unspoken,
As chipmunks declared, "Our party's unbroken!"
They danced to the rhythm of wind through the leaves,
Creating a ruckus that no one believes!

So tiptoe, dear friend, if you wish to explore,
Mind the lively hedge, or you'll join the uproar!
For the garden's alive, with a riotous tale,
And laughter will echo down each leafy trail!

The Lattice of Daydreams

In the lattice of dreams, where the flowers all scheme,
A ladybug spoke, saying, "Let's chase the moonbeam!"
The daisies all giggled, while the sun stretched his rays,
And the wind wrote a chorus, to lift up the praise.

A butterfly whispered, "I'll tell you a plan,
Let's throw a grand ball for the whole garden clan!"
With seeds in their pockets, they danced through the night,
As the crickets played music, a cheerful delight.

With ferns all a-flutter, and vines intertwining,
The garden grew tighter, with laughter defining.
They spun stories wildly, of cakes made of dirt,
And hats made of petals—a dapper dessert!

So come to the lattice, where fun knows no end,
Join the blooms in their games, allow laughter to bend.
In this whimsical garden, where dreams spin and weave,
You'll find that it's magic, if only you believe!

Fragrant Promises

Behind the bush, I found a cat,
Whispering secrets, just like that.
She promised me flowers, fresh and bright,
But all I got was a bug's delight.

The daisies giggled, the tulips danced,
In the sunlit bliss, they took a chance.
A snail in a tux, ready to race,
Said he'd leave the garden, just for a taste.

The roses claimed they knew the best brew,
But all they offered was morning dew.
With bees as bartenders, buzzing around,
I learned garden drinks were lacking sound.

So here's to the humor of nature's show,
Where laughter blooms wherever you go.
Among the petals, there's mischief and cheer,
A floral fiesta, that brings us near.

Nature's Invitation

In the forest, the trees wore hats,
With squirrels debating, and gossiping cats.
A feathered choir sang in delight,
While mushrooms concealed their party at night.

The daisies waved as I strolled on by,
Inviting me in with a wink of an eye.
I tripped on a root, fell into a stream,
And splashed a frog, who shouted, "Ice cream!"

The butterflies chuckled, flitting about,
As I fished for words in a puddle of doubt.
With every stumble, laughter would rise,
In a world where humor was the best prize.

So if you find laughter in nature's parade,
Follow the giggles, and be unafraid.
For every green nook holds a punchline or two,
An invitation to share joy anew.

Fibers of Time

In a web of vines, secrets entwine,
The spiders spin tales, quite divine.
But one old spider, known as Dave,
Told me his yarns were starting to cave.

With a wiggle and giggle, he'd weave away,
Laughing that time didn't care what we say.
A butterfly chimed in with a flutter,
"Time's just a story, not worth a clutter!"

The petals rolled their eyes, full of glee,
As history's tales laughed back at me.
The sun, it chuckled, casting bright rays,
For the garden knows how to fill up its days.

So weave your own stories, let laughter ring,
For the clock's just a fool, it can't make you sing.
In the fibers of time, with humor to find,
You'll see every moment is uniquely designed.

Hidden in the Vines

In the trellis, a parrot laid low,
Hiding from trouble, saying, "Oh no!"
A grape wrinkled up and quipped, "Don't you dare!"
"Not with my juice, will you give us a scare!"

Bunnies played tag in the zucchini patch,
While carrots were laughing, quite a good match.
But when the peas saw a shadow so grand,
They shrieked in delight, it was just a hand!

The vines intertwined, weaving their tales,
With dreams of wild dances in sunny trails.
Each leaf dripped with whimsy, ready to play,
In a garden that thrived on a bright, funny day.

So peek through the vines, you might just find,
A merry band of mischief, one of a kind.
For humor grows wild where the sun shines bright,
In a world of laughter, everything's right.

Reflections in the Trellis

In the trellis shadows, I found my shoe,
It's wearing a hat, and it's dancing too.
The daisies are giggling, they know my plight,
Those pesky squirrels are plotting tonight.

A snail in a top hat, he winks with glee,
He twirled past the roses, so pompously.
With every misstep, I trip and I sway,
Who knew the garden could lead me astray?

The gnomes by the fountain laugh with delight,
One thought he could fly, what a comical sight!
But splashing in puddles, he found his true calling,
While the tulips stood tall, no sign of falling.

As I wander and sway, with laughter in tow,
This garden's a circus, a delightful show.
With every few paces, a new joke I meet,
In the land of the garden, where humor's sweet.

Walk with the Wisteria

Beneath the wisteria, I took a stroll,
And bumped into bees in a dance-so-roll.
They buzzed a sweet tune, a laugh-filled delight,
As petals rained down, oh, what a sight!

An old tortoise chuckled, his shell all aflame,
He said, 'I'm not slow; I just play my own game!'
With each fragrant step, I stumbled and spun,
Who knew a garden could be so much fun?

The ivy whispered secrets with words full of cheer,
While frisky little rabbits kept darting near.
They offered me carrots, but I just ran away,
Giggling at antics that brightened my day.

So here in the garden, where laughter resides,
A tangle of joy in its vines and its tides.
Oh, walk with the wisteria, join in the spree,
Where whimsy and wonder refuse to flee.

Veil of Leaves

Behind a veil of leaves, I heard a loud quack,
A duck with a monocle, plotting a snack.
He offered me olives, proclaimed them gourmet,
I chuckled and nodded, then hurried away.

The flowers held meetings, conspiracies brewing,
Discussing the weather, and who they were wooing.
'What's that over there, is it food or a foe?'
They whispered of treasures, where the worms all grow.

An acorn slipped gossip, a tale of sweet seeds,
While ferns fanned themselves, discussing their needs.
Laughter erupted when a squirrel tripped light,
A tumble of twigs in the dazzling sunlight.

So under the canopy, fun is alive,
With chatter and chuckles, the garden will thrive.
So peek through the leaves, come bask in the glee,
Where joy is contagious, as lovely as can be.

The Arbor's Lament

Oh, the arbor stands strong, with a creak and a groan,
He sighs of the tales that from visitors flown.
With each raucous laugh, his bark becomes sore,
'Why must they all dance, and forget I'm a door?'

The vines braided stories, of silliness grand,
While the shadows held secrets, a mischievous band.
But who could resist, the charm in their fun?
Even the arbor, he yearns to run!

He dreams of the pranks the young sparrows will play,
A tug on a petal, then flutter away.
And yet with a creak and a chuckle, he sighs,
For laughter is fleeting, like clouds in the skies.

So I'll linger beneath him, hear all that I can,
For even old arbors can take part in the plan.
With jokes to be told, and stories to weave,
In this whimsical garden, it's hard not to believe.

Conversations with the Breeze

Whispers of wind in my hair,
The breeze tells jokes, breezy and rare.
It tickles the flowers, they giggle and sway,
Leaves laugh out loud, 'Come join our play!'

A butterfly winks, in on the jest,
It flutters around, really feeling blessed.
With every gust, a new tale unfolds,
Nature's humor is worth more than gold!

The daisies cheer, their petals so bright,
They dance in circles, a funny sight.
Even the rocks start cracking a grin,
As laughter blooms where the fun begins!

So let's all gather where laughter flows,
Beneath the sky where silliness grows.
The breeze carries cheer, it's so very neat,
In this garden of giggles, life feels complete!

The Color of Care

In hues of laughter, the flowers bloom,
Pink gives a wink, while yellow goes 'Zoom!'
Bluebells chuckle with shades so bold,
While green offers hugs, like stories retold.

Orange brings zest, with a zest for fun,
Violets giggle, 'Come join us, run!'
Every petal's a painter, slapping on cheer,
In this canvas of care, there's nothing to fear.

The sun shines down, a golden delight,
While jokes from the clouds keep floating in sight.
Rainbow connections, what a colorful flair,
Every splash of humor shows how much we care!

So let's splash some colors, and laugh 'til we drop,
In this garden of joy, let's never stop.
With every shade, our spirits repair,
Together we bloom, in the color of care!

Views from the Bower

From the old wicker chair, I take a peek,
Curious critters play hide and seek.
A squirrel tells stories, audibly grand,
As I sip my tea and give him a hand.

The sunflowers gossip, swaying so slow,
'Who wore it best?' they chatter and glow.
The lilacs laugh at their own perfume,
In the cozy bower, there's always room!

A rabbit hops by, with a jaunty flair,
He stops for a chat, 'Do you have some hair?'
We laugh at the thought, of a bunny on watch,
Who'd ever suspect he'd complain about a botch?

Each view from the bower, a tale to unfold,
Nature's comedians, never too old.
With petals and laughter and stories in sight,
In this funny garden, everything's right!

Tending the Heart

Water the heart with humor divine,
A sprinkle of giggles, it glows like a vine.
We prune off the worries, with snips of delight,
And plant seeds of laughter that sprout overnight.

Fertilize love with a pinch of good cheer,
With each funny memory, the garden draws near.
We chase away weeds, those thoughts that cause strife,
And giggle together at the bloom of our life.

Sunshine embraces, it tickles the soul,
With laughter and joy, we're perfectly whole.
In this patch of emotion, oh what a start,
With happy little stitches, we're tending the heart!

So here's to the laughter, let's make it our art,
In every small gesture, let kindness impart.
Together we flourish, with joy as our part,
In this lovely garden, we're tending the heart!

Symphonies of the Serene

In the morning light, the gnomes do sway,
As squirrels debate who'll steal the day.
Bees in a choir, they hum and buzz,
While daisies gossip about who loves.

Whispers of petals breathe in the breeze,
While butterflies flutter and tease the trees.
The fountain splashes with a giggly laugh,
As frogs conduct the symphony's path.

Sunflowers nod, "We've got endless flair!"
While the carrots argue, "Life's just unfair."
Together they dance, in colors so bright,
Nature's own joke, a whimsical sight.

Shadows in the Flowerbeds

Under the tulips, a shadow does creep,
A raccoon is plotting, where's he to leap?
In shadows they whisper, the flowers conspire,
"Who stole my sunlight, this thief of desire?"

Dandelions grumble, "We're weeds, not the best,"
While pansies wear frowns, in nature's jest.
Lilies roll eyes at the daffodil pride,
As bees form a band, in the chaos they glide.

Hiding below, a snail takes his time,
Dramatic and slow, in a shell so sublime.
While crickets share jokes, under the moon,
In flowerbed shadows, there's laughter at noon.

When Seasons Converge

When spring meets winter, it's quite a sight,
Ice skates on daisies, oh what a fright!
Pine trees having snowball fights with the bees,
While flowers wear sweaters, just for a tease.

The squirrels in jackets, maintaining their style,
Winter coats flapping, "We'll run for a mile!"
Giggles arise, from the branches above,
As nature's collage uncovers its love.

Rain dances with sunbeams, a quirky embrace,
As daffodils blush in this madcap space.
The wind plays a tune, from flower to tree,
While seasons collide, who knows what will be?

Fragments of Nature's Heart

Amidst the blooms, a secret is spun,
Laughter from petals as they bask in the sun.
Worms throw a party, in soil so fine,
With radishes ready to sip on some wine.

A ladybug dons tiny spectacles neat,
Sipping on dew drops, a gourmet treat.
While ants march in lines, a parade on the floor,
With tiny confetti from blossoms they score.

Fragrant whispers drift from the rose,
"Can you believe this? Watch how it grows!"
A playful breeze tickles, side to side,
Nature's own giggle, it cannot hide.